FAVOURITE ICE CREAM RECIPES

Ice Creams, Sorbets and Iced Puddings

compiled by
Carol Wilson

with illustrations by
George S. Elgood RI

SALMON

Index

Cover pictures: *front:* Montacute, Somerset *back:* Easton Lodge, Essex
title page: The Apollo, Balcaskie, Fife

Copyright, Printed and Published by J. Salmon Ltd., Sevenoaks, England ©

Fresh Coffee Ice Cream

Freshly ground coffee gives a superb rich, deep flavour to this delicious ice cream.

6 fl.oz very hot water
4 tablespoons fine ground
fresh coffee

6 egg yolks
8 oz light soft brown sugar
1 pint milk

Pour the water on to the ground coffee and leave to stand for 10 minutes. Strain the mixture to remove the coffee grounds. Combine the egg yolks and sugar in a heatproof bowl and whisk until very pale and thick. Whisk in the coffee and milk. Place the bowl over a pan of simmering (not boiling) water and cook, stirring all the time until the mixture is thick enough to coat the back of a wooden spoon. Remove from the heat and leave to cool, covering the surface with a piece of damp greaseproof paper to prevent a skin forming. Pour into a freezerproof container and freeze until half frozen. Remove from the freezer and whisk vigorously to prevent ice crystals forming. Repeat the process again then freeze until firm. Serves 4-6.

Raspberry Ripple Ice Cream

Sweet juicy raspberries are the taste of summer. Thawed, frozen raspberries can also be used to make a wonderful winter dessert.

2 oz flour	1 pint creamy milk
4 egg yolks	½ pint whipping cream
3 oz caster sugar	8 oz fresh raspberries
2 teaspoons vanilla extract	2 tablespoons icing sugar

Combine the flour, egg yolks, sugar and vanilla and stir in enough milk to give a thin paste. Heat the remaining milk and gradually stir into the paste, making sure there are no lumps. Pour into a pan and slowly bring to the boil, stirring all the time. Reduce the heat and cook gently for 3 minutes. Remove from the heat, cover with a piece of damp greaseproof paper to prevent a skin forming and leave until cold. Whisk the cream until thick but not stiff and fold into the cold custard. Transfer to a freezerproof container and freeze for 3-4 hours until partly frozen. Sieve the raspberries and stir in the icing sugar. Remove the ice cream from the freezer, beat it well and slightly swirl in the raspberry mixture to give a 'rippled' effect. Return the ice-cream to the freezer until solid. Transfer to the refrigerator 20-30 minutes before serving. Serves 6-8.

Honeycomb Crunch Ice Cream

A modern recipe which is quick and simple to make and contains crisp, puffy, golden toffee pieces.

1 pint whipping cream   2 tablespoons golden syrup
1 small tin condensed milk   5 tablespoons sugar
1 teaspoon bicarbonate of soda

Heat the sugar and syrup gently in a pan until melted, then boil for 3-4 minutes until a deep golden colour. Remove from the heat and stir in the bicarbonate of soda (the mixture will froth up) and immediately pour on to a greased tray to set. Whip the cream until thick but not stiff and fold in the condensed milk. Crush the honeycomb and fold the pieces into the cream mixture. Transfer to a freezerproof container. Cover and freeze. Use within 10 days. Serves 4.

Banana Custard Ice Cream

Use ripe bananas for the best flavour. Peel the bananas just before using and mix immediately with the lemon juice to prevent them discolouring.

1 tin (400g) condensed milk   **3 eggs, separated**
2 tablespoons custard powder   **4 bananas**
Juice of 1 lemon

Make up the condensed milk to 1½ pints with cold water. Blend the custard powder with a little of the milk to make a smooth paste. Heat the remaining milk in a pan to boiling point and pour on to the paste, mixing well. Return to the pan and bring to the boil again, stirring all the time and cook until the mixture thickens. Remove from the heat and allow to cool slightly. Beat the egg yolks and add the hot custard. Mash the bananas with the lemon juice and beat into the custard. Leave until cold, stirring occasionally. Pour into a freezerproof container, cover and freeze until just becoming firm. Turn the mixture into a bowl and beat well. Whisk the egg whites until stiff and fold into the ice cream. Return to the container, cover and freeze until firm. Place in the refrigerator about 30 minutes before serving. Serves 6.

Earl Grey Ice Cream

Earl Grey tea owes its delicate flavour to the addition of bergamot oil. The story goes that the recipe was given to the second Earl Grey in the nineteenth century by a Chinese mandarin, whose life had been saved by a British diplomat. It imparts a tantalising taste to this ice cream.

¼ **pint very strong Earl Grey tea**

¼ **pint creamy milk**	**3 egg yolks**
¼ **pint single cream**	**4 oz caster sugar**
Strip of lemon peel	¼ **pint whipping cream**

Put the tea, milk and single cream into a pan with the lemon peel and heat gently to simmering point. Remove from the heat. Whisk the egg yolks and sugar together until thick and pale, then whisk in the hot milk mixture. Discard the lemon peel and return the mixture to the pan and cook over a very low heat until the mixture thickens, but do not allow to boil or the mixture will curdle. Leave until cold, placing a piece of damp greaseproof paper on the surface. Pour into a freezerproof container, cover and freeze until half frozen. Turn into a bowl and whisk vigorously. Whip the cream until thick and fold into the mixture. Return to the container and freeze until firm. Place in the refrigerator half an hour before serving. Serves 6.

The Pergola, Great Tangley Manor, Surrey

Chocolate Parfait

*A parfait was originally a coffee flavoured dessert, but it has now come to mean
any light ice cream, which can be flavoured as preferred.*

¼ **pint water**	**3 tablespoons cocoa powder**
6 oz caster sugar	**2 oz plain chocolate, chopped**
½ **pint whipping cream**	

Place the water and sugar in a pan over a low heat until the sugar has dissolved.
Remove from the heat and sift in the cocoa powder. Bring to the boil slowly,
stirring all the time. Simmer gently for 5 minutes. Remove from the heat and add
the chocolate, stirring well. Leave to cool. Whisk the mixture until cold and thick
and chill in the refrigerator for 1 hour. Whip the cream until thick but not stiff and
gently fold into the chocolate mixture. Pour into a freezerproof container, cover
and freeze for at least 2 hours until firm. Transfer to the refrigerator 20 minutes
before serving. Serves 4.

Tutti-Frutti Ice Cream

The Italian 'tutti-frutti' literally means 'all fruits' and is used in Britain to describe an ice cream containing candied fruits.

4 oz sultanas	Strip of lemon peel
1 oz glacé cherries, chopped	4 tablespoons brandy or
1 oz crystallised pineapple, chopped	orange juice
1 oz candied peel, chopped	4 eggs, separated
Small piece angelica, diced	4 oz icing sugar
2 oz flaked almonds	½ pint double cream

Soak the fruits and lemon peel in the brandy or orange juice for at least 4 hours, or overnight. Whisk the egg yolks and sugar until thick and light. In another bowl, whisk the egg whites until stiff but not dry and fold into the yolk mixture. Pour into a freezerproof container and freeze until firm around the edges. Remove the lemon peel from the soaked fruit and discard. Remove the ice cream from the freezer and stir in the soaked fruits and their juices and the flaked almonds. Return to the container and cover and freeze until firm. Place in the refrigerator about 20 minutes before serving. Serves 6-8.

Fresh Mint Ice Cream

The fresh, clean taste of mint makes a refreshing ice cream which is ideal for a hot summer's day.

8 sprigs fresh mint   **12 fl.oz crème fraîche**
5 tablespoons caster sugar   **3 egg whites**

Chop the mint leaves finely and blend in the sugar, either in a blender or food processor or with a pestle and mortar, until well mixed. Stir into the crème fraîche. Whisk the egg whites until stiff but not dry and fold into the mint mixture. Place in a freezerproof container and freeze for at least 5 hours. Serves 6-8.

Chestnut Ice Cream

Made with tinned, sweetened chestnut purée, this ice cream is simple enough
for a child to make.

1 tin (225g) sweetened chestnut purée   **½ pint whipping cream**
2 tablespoons single cream or milk   **2 oz icing sugar**

Mix the chestnut purée with the single cream or milk to a smooth paste. Whip the cream with the sugar until thick but not stiff and fold into the purée. Turn into a freezerproof container, cover and freeze until firm. Serves 6.

Irish Cream Ice Cream

A rich, creamy ice cream. For a special occasion, serve scoops of Irish Cream ice cream in individual chocolate cases which are available from most large supermarkets.

1 pint double cream   **Pinch of salt**
2 oz icing sugar   **½ teaspoon vanilla essence**
3 tablespoons Irish Cream liqueur

Put all the ingredients into a bowl and whisk until thick. Pour into a freezerproof container, cover and freeze for 1 hour. Tip into a bowl and whisk to break down any ice crystals. Return to the freezer and repeat the process once more, then freeze until firm. Place in the refrigerator 20 minutes before serving. Serves 4-6.

Rich Vanilla Ice Cream

Vanilla, derived from the seed pods of a climbing orchid, native to the tropical forests of central America, reached Britain in the seventeenth century. By the early part of the twentieth century it had become an established flavouring for ice cream.

½ vanilla pod, split down the middle

3 oz sugar	**4 large egg yolks**
¾ pint whipping cream	**2 oz unsalted butter**

Place the sugar and cream in a pan over a low heat until the sugar has completely dissolved. Add the vanilla pod and bring to the boil. Remove from the heat, cover the pan and leave to stand for 25 minutes. Whisk the egg yolks lightly in a mixing bowl. Strain in the cream mixture, whisking all the time and return to the pan. Cook gently, stirring all the time, until the mixture thickens slightly, but do not allow it to boil or it will turn into scrambled eggs. Remove from the heat and stir in the butter. Pour into a freezer container and leave until cold. Cover and freeze for 1½ hours, then remove from the freezer and tip into a bowl and beat well. Return to the container and freeze until firm. Place in the refrigerator about 30 minutes before serving. Serves 4.

Butterscotch Ice Cream

Soft brown sugar and butter are cooked together to give a rich, toffee flavour to this delicious ice cream.

8 oz brown sugar **1¼ pints hot milk**
3 oz butter **4 egg yolks, beaten**

Melt the sugar and butter in a heavy pan and cook slowly until it begins to caramelise. Watch the mixture carefully to ensure that it does not become too dark or it will taste bitter. Remove from the heat and stir in the hot milk. Continue stirring until the toffee has dissolved completely. Cool slightly, then gradually pour on to the egg yolks in a heatproof bowl. Place the bowl over a pan of hot, but not boiling water, over a low heat and cook, stirring, until the custard is thick enough to coat the back of a spoon. Remove from the heat and leave to cool, stirring from time to time to prevent a skin forming. Place in a freezerproof container and freeze until half frozen. Remove from the freezer and tip into a bowl. Whisk vigorously to break down any ice crystals. Return to the freezer and repeat the process once more. Place in the refrigerator 30 minutes before serving. Serves 8.

Spiced Apple Ice Cream

Use well flavoured apples such as Cox's Orange Pippins, for an ice cream full of apple flavour.

1 lb apples, peeled, cored and sliced   **1 oz caster sugar**
2 oz butter   **2 eggs, separated**
2 tablespoons water   **¼ pint double cream**
2 cinnamon sticks, broken   **¼ pint single cream**

Place the apples, butter, water and cinnamon sticks into a pan and cook gently until soft. Remove from the heat and take out the cinnamon sticks. Add the sugar and beat to a purée. Whisk the egg yolks until frothy and stir into the purée. Return to the heat and cook over a low heat, stirring until the mixture thickens, but do not allow to boil. Pour into a bowl and leave to cool. Whisk the creams together in a bowl until thick and fold into the mixture. Turn into a freezerproof container and freeze for about 1 hour until half frozen. Turn out into a bowl. Whisk the egg whites until stiff but not dry and gently fold into the mixture. Return to the container and freeze until firm. Place in the refrigerator about 30 minutes before serving. Serves 4-6.

Crunchy Walnut Ice Cream

Frying the walnuts with butter, sugar and salt makes them deliciously crisp and crunchy.

4 oz walnuts, chopped roughly	**4 egg yolks**
2 oz butter	**4 oz caster sugar**
2 tablespoons granulated sugar	**½ pint milk**
2 teaspoons salt	**¼ pint double cream**

Melt the butter in a frying pan and add the nuts. Sprinkle on the sugar and salt and cook, stirring for 3-5 minutes until crisp. Remove from the heat and put to one side. Whisk the egg yolks and caster sugar together in a heatproof bowl. Heat the milk to simmering point, remove from the heat and pour on to the egg yolks, stirring all the time until blended. Place the bowl over a pan of simmering (not boiling) water and cook until thickened. Leave to cool. Pour into a freezerproof container, cover and freeze until becoming firm. Turn into a bowl and beat well. Gently fold in the cream and walnuts and spoon back into the container. Freeze until firm. Place in the refrigerator about 20 minutes before serving. Serves 4-5.

Fruity Rice Ice Cream

A rice ice cream appeared in Mrs. Marshall's Book of Ices in 1885. Not seen much in this country nowadays, it is still popular in Italy. This unusual ice cream is quickly made using a tin of rice pudding.

2 oz glacé cherries, chopped	**½ pint whipping cream**
2 oz candied peel, diced	**4 oz caster sugar**
3 fl. oz orange juice	**1 tin (450g) creamed rice pudding**

Soak the cherries and candied peel in the orange juice for a few hours. Stir into the remaining ingredients and chill the mixture. Place the mixture into a freezerproof container, cover and freeze until firm. Transfer to the refrigerator about 20 minutes before serving. Serves 8.

Rum and Raisin Ice Cream

Other dried fruits such as sultanas, currants, candied peel or a mixture can be used instead of the raisins. If no rum is to hand, substitute brandy or whisky instead.

6 oz raisins	**1 cinnamon stick, broken**
4 tablespoons rum	**3 eggs**
¾ pint creamy milk	**4 oz Demerara sugar**
¾ pint whipping cream	

Soak the raisins in the rum overnight. Next day, heat the milk in a pan with the pieces of cinnamon stick until almost boiling. Remove from the heat, cover and leave for 45 minutes, then remove the cinnamon pieces. Whisk the eggs and sugar until blended. Heat the milk again to just below boiling point and pour on to the egg mixture, whisking all the time. Return to the pan and cook over a low heat, stirring until the mixture thickens, but do not allow to boil. Remove from the heat and leave to cool, stirring occasionally. Whip the cream until thick, then fold into the custard with the raisins and any soaking liquor. Pour into a freezerproof container and cover and freeze until firm. Place in the refrigerator 30 minutes before serving. Serves 6-8.

Clotted Cream Ice Cream

Clotted cream is lusciously thick and rich and a glorious deep creamy yellow colour.
It has a minimum fat content of 55%. It is particularly associated with West Country
cream teas and makes a sumptuously rich ice cream.

¾ pint creamy milk   5 egg yolks
5 oz caster sugar   ¼ pint clotted cream
Few drops vanilla essence

Place the milk and half the sugar into a pan and heat gently until the sugar has dissolved. Heat until almost boiling. Beat the egg yolks with the rest of the sugar until thick and pale. Pour the hot milk in a steady stream on to the egg yolks, whisking all the time. Place the bowl over a pan of simmering (not boiling) water and cook, stirring, until thick enough to coat the back of a wooden spoon. Remove from the heat and leave to cool. Stir in the clotted cream and vanilla essence and leave until cold. Pour into a freezerproof container, cover and freeze until firm. Place in the refrigerator 20 minutes before serving. Serves 4-6.

Lemon Spoom

A spoom is a very light, fluffy ice cream. Lemon juice makes a very fresh tasting spoom.

2 fl. oz water   **Juice of 2 lemons**
4 oz sugar   **½ pint whipping cream**
2 egg whites

Heat the water and sugar in a small pan until the sugar has melted. Remove from the heat and allow to cool. Stir in the lemon juice and cream. Whisk the egg whites lightly until frothy and add to the mixture, mixing well. Pour into a freezerproof container, cover and freeze until firm. Serves 3-4.

Cinnamon Ice Cream

The warm fragrance of cinnamon makes an unusual ice cream with an intriguing flavour. Obtained from the inner bark of a tropical tree, cinnamon has been popular in this country since it was brought back from the Middle East in the 15th century.

1 pint milk	**8 oz caster sugar**
2 cinnamon sticks	**2 teaspoons ground cinnamon**
6 egg yolks	**½ pint whipping cream**

Heat the milk, cinnamon sticks and half the sugar in a pan to simmering point. Remove from the heat, cover and leave for at least 2 hours. Whisk the egg yolks with the remaining sugar until thick and light. Remove the cinnamon sticks from the pan and reheat the milk to simmering point. Pour in a thin stream on to the egg yolks, whisking all the time. Stir in the ground cinnamon, cover and chill overnight in the refrigerator to let the flavour develop. Stir in the cream and pour into a freezerproof container. Freeze until beginning to firm, then tip into a bowl and whisk vigorously. Return to the freezer. Place in the refrigerator about 25 minutes before serving. Serves 6.

Marmalade Ice Cream

To ring the changes, rather than using Seville orange marmalade, other types of marmalade such as ginger, grapefruit or tangerine can be used. Do not, however, use the sweet 'jelly' type marmalade as it makes the ice cream much too sweet.

1 pint single cream　　**8 oz dark, coarse cut Seville**
3 egg yolks　　　　　　　　**orange marmalade**
4 oz caster sugar　　**¼ pint double cream**

Place the single cream in a pan and heat to just under boiling point. Whisk the egg yolks and sugar together until fluffy, then whisk in the hot cream. Place the bowl over a pan of hot (not boiling) water and stir until the custard thickens and coats the back of a spoon. Remove from the heat and stir in the marmalade until it melts into the custard. Leave to become cold. Whip the double cream until thick but not stiff and fold into the cold custard. Spoon into a freezerproof container and freeze for at least 3 hours, beating the mixture twice during this time, to break down any ice crystals. Serves 6.

Brown Bread Ice Cream

A nineteenth century favourite. The breadcrumbs (which must be wholemeal) and sugar are caramelised into delicious sweet crunchy pieces.

4 oz Demerara sugar   4 oz wholemeal breadcrumbs   1 pint double cream
7 tablespoons rum or 1 teaspoon vanilla essence

Mix together the breadcrumbs and sugar and spread out on a greased baking tray. Place in the oven for 20-30 minutes, 375°F or Mark 5, stirring now and again with a fork. Leave to cool. Whisk the cream until soft peaks form, then gently fold in the rum or essence and cold, caramelised crumbs. Spoon into a freezerproof container, cover and place in the freezer until half frozen. Remove from the freezer and whisk vigorously to break down any ice crystals. Turn into a loaf tin lined with cling film and press down firmly. Cover and freeze until firm. Transfer the ice cream to the refrigerator about 30 minutes before serving. Serves 4-5.

Ginger Ice Cream

The spicy heat of this aromatic spice has been enjoyed in Britain for centuries. It is available ground, crystallised, candied in syrup or as a fresh root. This ice cream is especially delicious as an accompaniment to Christmas pudding.

4 fl.oz water	**½ pint double cream**
3 oz caster sugar	**3 oz stem ginger, finely chopped**
3 egg yolks	**1 tablespoon ginger syrup (from the jar)**

Heat the water and sugar in the pan over a low heat until the sugar has dissolved. Increase the heat and boil for 2-3 minutes until a little of the cooled syrup will form a thread when drawn between the thumb and forefinger (225°F/110°C on a sugar thermometer). Remove from the heat and cool slightly, then pour on to the egg yolks, whisking all the time until the mixture is thick and mousse-like. Whip the cream until thick but not stiff and fold in the ginger. Carefully fold the ginger cream into the mixture with the ginger syrup. Turn into a freezerproof container and freeze until firm. Place in the refrigerator 20 minutes before serving. Serves 4-6.

Honey Ice Cream

The luscious sweetness of honey produces a delectable ice cream. The flavour can be varied by experimenting with different types of honey, for example heather, lavender or orange blossom.

1 pint milk	**2 egg yolks**
1 vanilla pod	**6 oz clear honey**
2 eggs	**¼ pint double cream**

Place the milk and vanilla pod in a saucepan and heat gently until almost boiling. Cover and leave until lukewarm. Discard the vanilla pod and heat the milk again until hot but not boiling. Whisk the eggs and the yolks together in a heatproof bowl, then gradually whisk in the hot milk. Place the bowl over a pan of gently simmering (not boiling) water and stir all the time until the mixture is thick enough to coat the back of a wooden spoon. Set aside to cool, covering the top with a piece of damp greaseproof paper to prevent a skin forming. Warm the honey slightly and stir into the custard. Whip the cream lightly and fold into the mixture. Pour into a freezerproof container and freeze until half frozen. Remove from the freezer, whisk the mixture thoroughly and return to the freezer. Repeat the process once more, then freeze until firm. Serves 6.

Elderberry Sorbet

Sorbets or water ices were served at large dinner parties in Victorian and Edwardian times, between the entrée and the roast. The ice cold sorbet refreshed the palate so that the diners could continue through the remaining courses. Nowadays sorbets are also eaten as a refreshing dessert.

6 oz sugar	**1 lb elderberries**
½ pint water	**Squeeze of lemon juice**

Place the sugar and water into a heavy based saucepan and heat gently until the sugar is completely dissolved. Stir in the elderberries and simmer over a low heat until tender. Purée the mixture in a blender or rub through a sieve. Add the lemon juice to taste. Chill for 30 minutes. Pour into a freezerproof container, cover and freeze until firm, whisking well with a fork at 45 minute intervals. Half an hour before serving, place the sorbet in the refrigerator to soften slightly. Serves 4-6.

Blackberry Sorbet

Blackberries produce a beautifully coloured sorbet, which is ideal for an autumn dinner party.

1 lb blackberries	**½ pint water**
4 tablespoons water	**Finely grated rind and juice of 1 lemon**
4 oz caster sugar	**2 egg whites**

Place the blackberries and 4 tablespoons water in a pan and cook gently until soft; about 10 minutes. Rub through a sieve to remove the seeds. Place the sugar and ½ pint water in a pan and heat gently until the sugar has dissolved. Add the lemon rind and boil for 10 minutes. Leave to cool for at least 1 hour. Stir the lemon juice into the cooled syrup, followed by the blackberry purée. Pour into a freezerproof container and freeze for 3 hours. Remove from the freezer and tip into a bowl. Whisk the egg whites until stiff. Whisk the blackberry mixture with a fork and fold in the egg whites. Return to the freezer for at least 3 hours. Transfer to the refrigerator 30 minutes before serving. Serves 6.

Rose Sorbet

Roses, along with other edible flowers such as violets and lavender, were widely used in cookery in days gone by. This sorbet has the delicate scented flavour of roses. Use heavily scented rose petals, such as those of the damask rose, but make sure they are unsprayed and free from insecticides.

6 oz granulated sugar   **4 oz rose petals**
¾ pint water   **Pink colouring**
Juice of 1 lemon   **Rose water**
2 egg whites

Heat the sugar and water over a low heat until the sugar has dissolved. Add the lemon juice and bring to the boil. Simmer for 10 minutes. Remove the bitter white 'heel' from the base of the rose petals, then pour the hot syrup over the rose petals, cover and leave until cold. Place in a blender or processor and work until almost smooth. Sieve the mixture into a bowl and add the colouring and rose water to taste. Pour into a container, cover and freeze until slushy. Turn the mixture into a bowl and beat well. Whisk the egg whites until stiff but not dry and fold into the mixture. Return to the container, cover and freeze until firm. Place in the refrigerator 15 minutes before serving. Serves 6.

Melon Sorbet

Any type of ripe melon can be used in this sorbet; for example galia, charentais, cantaloupe, etc.

2 lbs melon   **4 egg whites**
Juice of ½ lemon   **4 oz caster sugar**

Remove the rind and seeds from the melon and cut the flesh into chunks. In a food processor or blender work the melon with the lemon juice until smooth. Turn into a freezerproof container and freeze until just starting to set around the edges. Remove from the freezer and tip into a bowl. Beat the egg whites until stiff, then gradually whisk in the sugar until the mixture is stiff and shiny. Whisk the melon mixture and fold in the egg whites. Return to the freezer container and freeze until firm; about 3 hours. Leave to stand at room temperature for 10 minutes before serving. Serves 6-8.

Lemon Sorbet

Sorbets made from citrus fruits are especially refreshing and cooling in hot weather.

1 pint water	**Thinly pared rind and juice**
2 teaspoons powdered gelatine	**of 3 lemons**
10 oz caster sugar	**2 egg whites**

Put 2 tablespoons water into a small cup and sprinkle on the gelatine; leave to soak for 5 minutes. Put the remaining water, sugar and lemon rinds into a pan and heat gently, stirring until the sugar has completely dissolved. Bring to the boil, lower the heat and simmer for 5 minutes. Remove from the heat, cool slightly and add the soaked gelatine, stirring until dissolved. Add the lemon juice and leave to become quite cold. Strain the syrup into a freezerproof container and freeze, uncovered, until slushy. Whisk the egg whites until stiff. Place the half frozen mixture into a bowl, add the whisked egg whites and whisk until thick. Return to the container and freeze for several hours until firm. Serve straight from the freezer. Serves 8.

White Wine Sorbet

This is a sophisticated dessert which is definitely for adults only!

1 lb caster sugar   **½ pint sweet white wine, e.g. Sauterne**
1 pint water   **Juice of 2 lemons**
Juice of 1 orange

Place the sugar, water and wine in a pan and heat gently until all the sugar has dissolved. Bring to the boil and cook for 5 minutes. Set aside and leave to cool for at least 1 hour then stir in the fruit juices. Pour into a freezerproof container and freeze until firm. Serves 4-6.

Pear Sorbet

Pears make a refreshing, fruity sorbet. Choose a well flavoured variety such as Comice, Bartlett or William. Start this recipe the day before it is needed.

2 oz butter	12 oz sugar
2 lbs pears	1½ pints water
4 oz soft brown sugar	Finely grated rind and juice 3 lemons
1 tablespoon brandy (optional)	1 egg white
¼ pint double cream	

Melt the butter in a large pan. Peel, core and slice the pears. Add the brown sugar, 1 tablespoon lemon juice and the pears to the pan and cook gently until the mixture 'falls' and the fruit is soft. Cool and rub through a sieve into a bowl. Cover and chill overnight. Heat the sugar, water, lemon rind and juice in a pan until the sugar has dissolved. Bring to the boil and simmer for 12 minutes. Transfer to a freezerproof container and freeze overnight. Next day, turn into a bowl and beat well, then beat in the pear purée, egg white and double cream. Return to the freezer for at least 8 hours until firm. Serves 4-6.

Raspberry Yoghurt Sorbet

This recipe makes a smooth, creamy sorbet. Do not use low fat yoghurt or the finished dish will be hard and icy; Greek style yoghurt is ideal.

½ lb raspberries
2 cartons (150g) natural yoghurt
1 tablespoon powdered gelatine

3 tablespoons cold water
2 egg whites
3 oz caster sugar

Blend the raspberries to a smooth purée and rub through a sieve to remove the seeds. Stir in the yoghurt. Sprinkle the gelatine over the water in a small bowl and when it 'sponges' heat gently by standing the bowl in a pan of hot (not boiling) water until dissolved, then add to the purée. Whisk the egg whites until stiff, then gradually whisk in the sugar. Fold the meringue gently into the purée and turn into a freezerproof container. Cover and freeze until firm. Transfer to the refrigerator 30 minutes before serving. Serves 4-6.

Chocolate Marquise

A marquise is a very rich, dark, frozen chocolate dessert, with the consistency of a smooth mousse. Serve it with coffee sauce or a cold, creamy custard sauce.

8 oz good quality plain chocolate
4 oz unsalted butter

2 large eggs, separated
Pinch of salt
3 oz icing sugar

Break up the chocolate into a heatproof bowl and add the butter. Heat gently over a pan of simmering (not boiling) water until the mixture has melted and is smooth. Whisk the egg whites with the salt until stiff. Whisk the egg yolks with the sugar until pale and creamy. Lightly mix the melted chocolate mixture into the egg yolk mixture, then fold in the whisked whites. Spoon into a 2 lb loaf tin lined with cling film or non-stick baking paper and cover with foil. Freeze until firm. Turn out just before serving and cut into slices. Serves 4-6.

Country House Iced Pudding

Frozen confections were described as 'iced puddings' and were very fashionable during the 1920s and 30s, when more households acquired refrigerators. In this recipe, for simplicity and speed, a ready made cake is substituted for a cake made in a loaf tin.

A 1 lb Madeira cake   1 dessertspoon caster sugar
½ pint double cream   8 tablespoons sherry or brandy
4 oz glacé cherries, quartered

Split the cake lengthways into 3 slices. Line a 1 lb loaf tin with cling film. Whip the cream and sugar with 1 tablespoon sherry or brandy to stiff peaks. Place one slice of cake in the base of the loaf tin and sprinkle with one third of the remaining sherry or brandy. Cover with half the cream and half the remaining sherry or brandy. Top with a slice of cake. Cover with the rest of the cream and the cherries. Top with the remaining cake and sprinkle with the rest of the sherry or brandy. Cover with foil and freeze for at least 4 hours. Turn out just before serving and cut into slices to serve. Serves 6-8.